BULLETPROOF SOUL

Jennifer Farmer

BULLETPROOF SOUL

OBERON BOOKS
LONDON

WWW.OBERONBOOKS.COM

First published in 2007 by Oberon Books Ltd
521 Caledonian Road, London N7 9RH
Tel: +44 (0) 20 7607 3637 / Fax: +44 (0) 20 7607 3629
e-mail: info@oberonbooks.com
www.oberonbooks.com

PB ISBN: 9781840027310
E ISBN: 9781786823229

Cover design by Fluidesign

Characters

DAD, 50

DOCTOR, 60

SOL WALKER, 23

RENA WALKER, 17

OSCAR PARSONS, 60

ALICE KWAGALA, 17

UNCLE YUSEFU, 55

For a cast of 5, the following can be doubled:

DAD / UNCLE YUSEFU

DOCTOR / OSCAR PARSONS

Notes on the text:

If there is no dialogue after a character's name, this indicates an active silence between the characters. This is where characters can also take a moment to make a transition.

A slash ' / ' indicates overlapping of dialogue – the point at which the next character starts speaking.

Bulletproof Soul was first performed on 1 March 2007 at The Door, Birmingham Rep, with the following company:

DAD / UNCLE YUSEFU, John Adewole
DOCTOR / OSCAR PARSONS, Patrick Romer
SOL WALKER, Nick Oshikanlu
RENA WALKER, Cassie Joseph
ALICE KWAGALA, Demi Oyediran

Director Natasha Betteridge
Designer Bernadette Roberts
Composer Tayo Akinbode
Vocal Coach Sally Hague
Lighting Designer Barry Hope
Production Manager Thomas Wright
Stage Manager Kelly Hodder
Deputy Stage Manager Emma Ledsum

The author thanks Natasha Betteridge, Carl Miller and everyone at the Rep for their support and patience; Micheline Steinberg, Matt Connell and Helen MacAuley at Micheline Steinberg Associates; Tim Ford and the Young Rep; The Peggy Ramsay Foundation.

SCENE 1

A hospital ward.

There is a sense that there are a number of other patients on the ward.
DAD sits on an empty, unmade bed. SOL stands.

DAD: I mean, Uganda, Sol? People here need help; your
mother and I need help. You go from country to country;
does it take your mother having a stroke to get you to stay
more than a few days at a time? Your sister's no better,
not with her in and out of trouble. Don't let me get started
on that girl. If it weren't for her, we could have been...
(*Beat.*) You say you want to help people. 'I want to make
a difference, Dad.' But when will that be? Your mum and
me, we'll be dead and buried by the time you make a
difference. (*Beat.*) You're twenty-three, Sol. When are you
going to come home and get a job? A proper job. (*Beat.*)
'Capacity-building'; what is that, Sol? I don't speak jargon.
'Capacity-building'. I speak English. And don't tell me
that's a proper job. Boy, you don't know what a proper
job is. You don't have to like a proper job, but a proper
job pays a proper wage. Charity work doesn't pay proper
wages. Charity work –

DOCTOR enters, checking his notes. DAD stands up to greet
him.

DOCTOR: Mr Walker?

DAD: Yes.

They shake hands.

DOCTOR: Doctor Green. I just wanted to update you on your
wife's latest test results. The stroke doesn't seem to have
caused much paralysis, but she will need physiotherapy to
strengthen that right side. You can get someone to come
out to you or there's the out-patient option. Whatever is
more convenient. Not everyone, I know, is comfortable

with people coming into their homes. Do you have any support at home?

DAD scoffs.

Kids have all flown the nest, have they? Great when that happens, isn't it? (*To SOL.*) No offence.

SOL extends his hand and they shake.

SOL: Sol.

DOCTOR: And you aren't at home, I take it?

DAD kisses his teeth.

SOL: No; I work abroad.

DOCTOR: International banking? Goldman Sachs; J P Morgan?

DAD: If only.

SOL: Helping Hands. I teach English on capacity-building projects.

DOCTOR: Oh, yeah? We've had interns that had placements with Helping Hands. Costa Rica. India. Where was Nicole; the Democratic Republic of Congo – no, the Dominican Republic, sorry. The Dominican Republic. Someone just came back from Sudan; who was that? Who was that? It will come to me later. So, where have you been?

DAD: Over there with them Arabs.

SOL: (*To DAD.*) Palestine.

DAD: We have Arabs here.

SOL: (*To DOCTOR.*) India; the Dharamsala region and Bhopal.

DAD: Got them too.

SOL: Just off the plane from Cambodia.

DAD: I'm sure we got some of them, whatever they are.

Beat.

DOCTOR: When I was a lad, a group of us travelled to Saigon. Will never forget the taste of deep-fried spiders. But that was donkey's ago. It's changed since then; for the better, I hope. (*Beat.*) That's a lot of travelling for a young man of...

SOL: Twenty-three.

DOCTOR: Twenty-three?! At twenty-three I was trying to figure out why chasing girls and medical school didn't mix. Mr Walker, you must be proud.

DAD: Hmm...

DOCTOR: Where to next?

SOL: Uganda. I'm overseeing the setting up of a school out there; kind of a promotion.

DOCTOR: Uganda, huh? Do you know Africa well?

SOL: This will be my first placement in Africa, actually.

DOCTOR: Really? That's a surprise. I mean, I thought Africa would be the first place you would want to go.

SOL: Why?

DOCTOR:

SOL:

DOCTOR: Uh...I don't know, really. I just assumed... You know, kids today, they need a role model like you. To show them that it's not all about guns and gangs.

SOL: What kids?

DOCTOR: Well, like the kid, the Black kid that came in not three hours ago; gunshot wound. DOA. They said he was in the wrong place at the wrong time, but I mean you just know he wasn't that innocent. Now if he had somebody to look up to... (*Pause.*) Gun crime is really destroying the Black community, isn't it? But hopefully you'll sort it out.

Silence.

SOL: I'm not the Black community.

DAD sighs.

DOCTOR: Of course not.

Silence.

Well, good luck in Uganda. (*To DAD.*) Remember; Mrs Walker needs plenty of rest and as little stress as possible. I'll leave details about the physio with the duty nurse.

DOCTOR exits, and as he does so RENA is seen listening in on the other side of the curtain. Neither DAD nor SOL notices her.

Beat.

DAD: I can't believe you; back-chatting a doctor!

SOL: What, Dad? He –

DAD: He's a doctor. And why did you tell him that? 'Capacity-building?' Don't say that, don't tell people that, say something else, like – I don't know – that you're a head teacher. Or a professor.

SOL: But 'capacity-building' is what I do.

DAD: And do you have to stand there, talking to the doctor, looking the way you do? Look at you. What do you look like?

SOL looks down at his clothes.

SOL: It's hemp.

DAD: You look a tramp. I didn't pay for a first-rate education so you can wear second-hand clothes.

Silence. SOL notices RENA, who smiles smugly at him.

Your mum and me, we didn't work all the hours God sent so our children can walk around like they don't got the sense they were born with.

RENA saunters in, eating from a packet of crisps. As soon as she enters, DAD stiffens. RENA flops down on the hospital bed.

RENA: God this is lumpy.

RENA bounces up and down on the bed, jostling DAD, who has his eyes clenched shut. SOL is about to say something, but changes his mind. RENA continues to bounce on the bed. SOL notices how angry DAD is becoming.

SOL: Rena…

RENA: It's a wonder if Mummy can sleep. I couldn't sleep on this thing. Couldn't you get her a private room or something? When's she coming home?

SOL: In a few days.

RENA: You really should have gone private. When can I see her?

SOL: Mum can't be stressed, Rena.

RENA: Who's stressing her? I just want to see my mum, yeah? Is she coming home tonight, Dad?

SOL: Rena, Mum needs –

RENA: (*Pointedly.*) Dad?

Silence. She holds out the crisps to DAD, ignoring SOL. DAD locks eyes on RENA. Long pause.

What? You don't like cheese and onion or something?

DAD knocks the crisps from RENA's hand.

Oi, what you do that for?! Them crisps cost me seventy-five p!

DAD: Keep that girl away from me, hear Sol, before I break her neck!

RENA: What? What I do?

DAD: 'What I do?'! Her mother's in hospital because of her shenanigans –

RENA: Ay, don't blame / Mummy's stroke on me!

DAD: Her goings-on and all she has to say for herself is, 'What I do?'!

RENA: I weren't even there when it happened! And neither were you!

DAD: No, because I was collecting you from the police station; again. I would have been able to help her. Instead, I'm waiting for them to bring you up when your mother's lying on the floor. She's lying there, alone, on her own kitchen floor.

RENA: Everyone blame Rena. (*To SOL.*) What about you, huh?

SOL: Nobody has to pick me up from the police station.

RENA: No, coz you ain't never in the country. You ain't never home. Where were you?

SOL: I was helping people.

RENA: 'Where you coming from this time, Sol?' 'Oh, I'm just in from Oompa Loompa Land.' 'That's nice. Isn't Sol nice?' 'A nice lad?' So where were you when Mummy got sick? (*Beat.*) Why don't you just go, yeah? Just smack it, Sol, coz we don't need you.

SOL: Don't worry, Rena. I'll be out of here in a few days' time.

DAD: If you're going, then you'd better take her.

RENA: Take who?

SOL: Sorry?

DAD: No stress for your mum, the doctor said.

RENA: Me? I don't need no babysitter.

DAD: She can't take any more. I can't –

RENA: Where? Nah-uh, man. Forget it.

DAD: You want to help people; charity begins at home, Sol. (*Beat.*) When your mother comes out of hospital, I want her gone.

RENA: Gone?! That's my home, too!

DAD exits.

SOL: Dad, please...

RENA: I'll squat on a mate's floor before I go with this fool.

SCENE 2

Schoolhouse, Uganda.

The schoolhouse is an old disused building; an empty shell of a space. As yet, there are no chairs, tables or desks.

SOL is unpacking second-hand textbooks and supplies. RENA sits on an unopened box, fanning herself. SOL, struggling with a load of supplies, drops a stack of pencils and they scatter everywhere. RENA laughs maliciously as SOL bends down to pick them up. As he does so, he drops a ream of paper that he is holding. RENA laughs even harder.

SOL: You could help.

Beat. RENA kicks the pencil nearest her over to SOL. Beat.

RENA: The word is 'thank you'.

SOL: If you hadn't kept bunking off school, you'd know that's two words, actually.

RENA gives SOL the two-fingered salute.

Charming.

SOL continues to collect the scattered pencils and paper.

(*To himself.*) This is for Mum, this is for Mum, this is for Mum.

RENA: What, picking up paper off the floor? (*Beat.*) Come off it, bruv. We both know that I could've crashed at one of my spars'.

SOL is busy counting the pencils.

I could've, man. I just wanted to vex you by coming out here. (*Beat.*) I did. And Dad, well he thought it would be good for me to get away for a bit. Coz Dad knows the kind of stress I've been under lately. And the only reason Dad didn't come to the airport was coz he's not one for tearful goodbyes.

RENA watches as SOL remains engrossed in his task.

You know, you shouldn't crawl on the floor like that, getting your trousers dirty. But then again, what do you care that Mum and Dad didn't pay for a first-class education so you can wear second-hand clothes.

Pause. RENA knows SOL's heard her. RENA walks over to the doorway, stepping on sheets of paper and breaking several pencils in the process. SOL tries to get as much stuff as he can out of her path.

SOL: What the hell are you doing?!

RENA: They were in my way.

SOL: Do you know how precious this is?!

RENA shrugs.

RENA: Just look like pencils and paper to me.

SOL: These donations will have to last the whole year.

RENA: Better keep them off the floor then.

Beat. SOL shakes his head is disbelief and continues to gather everything up.

What these Africans need to be learning about is air-con, man. I mean, I thought we were making poverty history! What was *Live 8* for, then? It ain't like there wasn't like millions of us watching the show. You think with all the help we gave them, cancelling debts and all that they'd be grateful enough to buy some kind of cooling system. You'd think they'd –

SOL: Rena?

RENA: What?

SOL: Please be quiet.

RENA: What, can't I state my opinion?

SOL: No.

RENA: Why?

SOL: Because no one wants to hear it, okay?

RENA: Fascist.

SOL: Oooo, big word for you, Rena.

RENA: I've got an even bigger one; 'prick'. (*Beat.*) Where the fans at?! I can't buy a breeze up in here.

SOL: You don't even realise when someone is doing you a favour, do you?

RENA: Nah-uh, unlike your savage charity cases, I don't need your handouts.

SOL: No? Your 'spars' wouldn't even let you kip on their floor. Now what's that say about you?

RENA:

OSCAR enters.

OSCAR: I hope this is where all the fun's happening. That Kate, she's doing my head in with all that admin.

OSCAR holds out his hand.

Oscar Parsons – Wait, I remember you. I've worked with you before, right? Where was it? Tibet?

A stunned SOL scrambles to stand up, pencils and paper still in hand.

SOL: Palestine.

OSCAR: Palestine, that's it. (*Beat.*) Youngblood, right?

SOL: Sol. Walker. (*Beat.*) Youngblood. That's what you called me.

OSCAR: May forget a place, but I never forget a nickname. How's it going?

OSCAR shakes SOL's hand vigorously.

SOL: Okay, I guess. I didn't, I didn't expect to see you again.

OSCAR: No one ever does in my case.

SOL: I thought Palestine was to be your last gig.

OSCAR grunts.

OSCAR: Thought I'd make Uganda my last shout. I'm really too old for this shit.

SOL: Yes, Uganda – what a coincidence.

OSCAR: If you believe in that sort of thing. And I don't. You just arrive?

SOL: Two days ago. You?

OSCAR: Just over three weeks ago. Hitched my way from Kampala. Just wanted to have a look at the country before we got stuck in. (*To RENA.*) And who is this?

SOL: Uh…

RENA: Rena.

OSCAR: Pleasure's all mine, Rena. Oscar.

RENA: I heard.

OSCAR: So Rena, are –

SOL: Long time since Palestine. What three years?

OSCAR: Yeah, about that. I remember now. Israeli tanks didn't put you off humanitarian aid, I see. (*To RENA.*) First time I laid eyes on Youngblood here, he was standing in front of a bulldozer, about to raze the school to the ground.

SOL: You know…

OSCAR: It worked; the school was left standing. So where did you two meet? It's not unheard of for romance to blossom over anti-malaria tablets.

RENA: What?! No, no, no, no, hell no! Man, he's my brother.

OSCAR: Ahh. (*Beat. To SOL.*) So is this the sister?

OSCAR clicks his fingers, trying to remember something.

What is it? What is it? (*To RENA.*) Menia zovut Oscar. Rad s vamee poznakomit'sya.

Pause as OSCAR waits for RENA to respond. SOL is about to say something but realises it's too late.

Did I get that right? I didn't, did I? Here's me trying to blind you with the only bit of Russian I know. Learned it from a girl I was working with in Guatemala. So, how would you say: 'Which writers have captured the zeitgeist of the nation?'

RENA: How should I know?

OSCAR laughs, thinking RENA's made a joke. He quickly realises that she hasn't.

OSCAR: When Sol mentioned you studied in Moscow, I assumed you'd be fluent in the native language. Anyway, please tell me you find Dostoevsky overrated. I say that, people think I'm mad.

RENA: I can see why.

OSCAR: I'm a Pushkin man, myself. Who do you like?

Silence as OSCAR waits for RENA to respond. The waiting becomes uncomfortable.

Gogol? Tolstoy? Turgenev? Don't say Chekhov, everyone says Chekhov.

RENA: What are you on about?

OSCAR: Just thought you could give me a few tips. I am in the presence of a scholar of Russian Literature.

RENA: What?

OSCAR: Don't be modest; I hate people that are modest – it's a waste of time. A scholar of Russian is what you are.

RENA: Nah-uh. I ain't studied Russian anything, mate.

OSCAR: Really? You sure?

RENA shakes her head.

Sol said he had a sister that studied in Moscow.

RENA: I bet he did.

OSCAR: I thought that might be you.

RENA: Nope.

OSCAR: Sorry. Must be your other sister, then.

RENA: There ain't no other sister.

OSCAR looks at SOL.

OSCAR:

SOL:

RENA: Just me.

Beat.

OSCAR: I'm sure it was Youngblood that – sorry, I must've gotten the wrong end of the stick.

RENA: Uh-huh.

OSCAR: Uhm, anyway, pleased to meet you, Rena. How are you liking Uganda so far?

RENA: I'm not.

SOL: What she means is that the lack of infrastructure…I mean by the civil war and…she's overwhelmed.

OSCAR: Yeah, is a bit of a mess, isn't it? So, where else have you been on placement?

RENA: Place –

SOL: This is Rena's first time – in a placement abroad.

OSCAR: Well enjoy it. (*Beat.*) So Youngblood, fill me in. What else you been up to? What other civil unrest are you causing?

SOL: Well uhm, there was a demo against the Terrorism Act a few days ago.

OSCAR: Good turnout?

Beat.

SOL: I, uhm, I missed it, actually.

OSCAR: From what I remember, you're not one to miss a demonstration. As I recall, you were always organising one.

SOL: Family troubles. Our mum, she had a stroke.

OSCAR: Oh, I'm sorry. I'm very sorry to hear that.

SOL: She'll be fine; our dad's there. Rena's with me to give Mum some space.

OSCAR: It must be a comfort to have a good lad like you.

RENA rolls her eyes.

Bet you had your heart set on that demo, huh?

RENA: Not –

SOL: Rena doesn't get caught up in politics.

OSCAR: Really? That's a surprise.

RENA: Actually Oscar, I've been –

SOL: But she's starting to get an awareness.

OSCAR: It's never too late to get your political bearings. I didn't sign my first petition until I was at uni.

SOL: I was eight.

RENA: Of course you were.

OSCAR laughs.

OSCAR: Has he always been so headstrong?

RENA: If that's what you wanna call it, then yeah.

OSCAR: Always the provocateur.

RENA: Always the –

SOL: I just try to do what I can when I see an injustice.

RENA: Oh God…

SOL: I think this will be a real eye-opener. For all of us.

OSCAR: I must admit even I'm feeling a bit –

RENA: Hot?

OSCAR: Apprehensive. And I've seen some shit. But these poor kids. That sounds so patronising, I know. But…fuck me, did they ever get to be children? Did they get to have a childhood?

SOL: Childhoods were stolen from them by corrupt governments and authorities; people who should have known better.

OSCAR: Right?

OSCAR looks at RENA, who shrugs.

RENA: I haven't a clue as to what you're on about.

OSCAR: The students.

RENA: What students?

SOL: The ones we're here to teach.

RENA: What about them?

OSCAR: The fact they used to be soldiers.

RENA: What?!

OSCAR: You didn't know?

RENA: Nah-uh.

OSCAR: Unbelievable, I know.

RENA: For real? They used to blatt, blatt, blatt?

RENA mimes shooting a gun. Beat.

SOL: Yes.

RENA: They really killed people?

SOL: Yes.

RENA: Straight-up gangsta.

SOL: Rena, please.

RENA: Hopefully some of the blokes'll be fit.

SOL: Rena!

RENA: What? (*To OSCAR.*) How old are these killing machines then?

Beat as OSCAR looks a bit unsure at her choice of phrase.

OSCAR: Some in their teens. A few are twenty, twenty-one. Some might be twelve or even younger.

RENA: What, twelve?! How can they join the army if they're twelve?

SOL: Don't you watch the news?

RENA: Not really.

SOL: Not really.

OSCAR: The rebel army's illegal, that's why they can have children fight.

SOL: If you paid attention to what goes on in the world, you'd know this.

RENA: What I do?

SOL: Nothing, that's the problem.

RENA: You can have a go at me, but least I ain't got nobody shot up. (*Beat.*) Well, not that I know of.

SOL: They are not silly kids playing at 'keeping it real'. These are victims, Rena. Victims of corruption and manipulation who –

RENA: Who killed people and that's not right. Is it, Oscar?

OSCAR: No, it's not, Rena.

RENA: (*To SOL.*) And you said I wasn't into politics.

SOL: You –

RENA: Oscar, did you know I've even been arrested; for protesting? Exercising my freedom of assembly.

OSCAR: Alright, Lil' Sis.

SOL: Well –

RENA: A political prisoner, me. Just before we came out here. Sol ain't the only Walker that can organise a 'demo'.

OSCAR shakes his head.

OSCAR: And they say young people are apathetic.

RENA: It was well worth it, getting banged up.

OSCAR: No shame in getting incarcerated in the name of your beliefs.

RENA: True that.

OSCAR: Sometimes, that's the only way us little people can be heard.

RENA: Exactly.

OSCAR: Because when we break down the walls of that cage they call a prison cell, the whole world will hear our cry.

RENA: Let the church say 'Amen!'

OSCAR: So what was the cause, warrior?

SOL: It was nothing, Oscar.

OSCAR: (*To RENA.*) What were you fighting for?

SOL: Rena doesn't –

OSCAR: Sol, let the woman speak.

RENA: Yeah Sol, let the woman – let me speak. (*To OSCAR.*) Me and my spars, right, we was getting pretty vexed about the whole Somali situation.

OSCAR: Oh man. It's so good to know people are looking beyond the racism and xenophobia of the media.

RENA: You what? Nah, we was protesting that the asylum seekers is taking over. You can't move for all them foreigners. What about our housing and our benefits? Our jobs? Who's looking out for us? Don't seem like the council was listening, so we decided to get the message across ourselves. They heard us that time.

OSCAR: Sorry?

RENA: We threw stones at them freeloaders. You shoulda seen it, yeah? Black and White kids together. A few Asian lads. Fighting for our country, innit.

Beat.

OSCAR: You were chucking rocks *at* the Somali kids?

RENA: Believe.

OSCAR: At other Black kids?

RENA: No, we're Black; they're Somali. (*Beat.*) Nobody got hurt. Not hurt bad, anyway. We was the ones that came out of it worst. You shoulda heard what them lot was calling us. They gave just as good as they got. Now they know not to be using our community centre.

OSCAR: Your community centre?

RENA: We were there first! And don't go giving me that mouthful about them fleeing war and poverty. Man, I seen war! At the post office, you try staying too long at the window on giro day! A bloodbath!

RENA laughs.

OSCAR: I've got work to get on with.

OSCAR walks off.

SOL: Let me give you a hand, Oscar.

SOL exits. RENA calls after them.

RENA: Nah, but you don't wanna hear that, do you?! You don't wanna hear our side of things!

RENA is left on her own. She walks around the empty schoolhouse and steps on an already broken pencil that SOL missed – crushing the pencil further. RENA picks up the pencil and tries to connect the broken ends, but the pencil is beyond repair. RENA becomes frustrated with trying to make the ends fit so she breaks the pencil into as many smaller pieces as she can.

ALICE, carrying a satchel, enters and watches RENA's pencil-breaking frenzy.

ALICE: That's why I like pens.

RENA is startled by ALICE.

(*Knowing she isn't late.*) I hope I am not late.

RENA shrugs.

I like to be early. And prepared.

ALICE notices the mess.

And neat.

ALICE takes several books out of her satchel and places them on top of the pile of paper and pencils that SOL collected from the floor.

Song of Lawino. Abyssinian Chronicles. Return to the Shadows. Tensions. Weep Not, Child. I know that Ngugi wa Thiong'o is really Kenyan, but he did study his writing in Uganda. (*Beat.*) No? Or maybe, Mary Karooro Okurut's *A Woman's Voice*? With which shall we begin?

Pause.

Or do you have titles that you can suggest?

RENA shakes her head. ALICE waits.

RENA:

ALICE:

RENA:

Beat.

ALICE: Sol Walker?

RENA shakes her head.

Ahh. So you are not the teacher.

RENA: Nope.

ALICE: Good. You do not talk enough to be a teacher.

Beat.

RENA: He'll be back.

ALICE: Okay.

Pause. ALICE extends her hand.

Alice Kwagala.

RENA hesitates before taking her hand. They shake. ALICE holds RENA's hand long after the end of the handshake. RENA becomes visibly uncomfortable, which ALICE notices so releases her hand.

It is our custom. You will get used to it.

RENA: That's okay. I'm Rena. Walker.

ALICE: It is a pleasure to meet the teacher's wife.

RENA: Sister, sister, alright?!

ALICE: Sister, okay. (*Beat.*) British, yes?

RENA: Londoner.

ALICE smiles. This causes RENA to smile – but just a little one.

ALICE: My friend, her auntie, she lives in… (*Hesitates.*) … Dalston?

RENA: East London girl. (*Points to herself.*) Stratford.

ALICE: The Olympics!

RENA: Yeah!

They laugh.

Except they're knocking down our community centre to build something or other; some complex or arena or something. But that's okay. That's alright. Roll on 2012.

ALICE looks confused.

You got good English.

Beat.

ALICE: Uhh, thank you.

RENA: Not like them Somali.

ALICE: I am Ugandan.

RENA: Yeah, but you're – never mind.

ALICE: I am –

She is interrupted by SOL's voice.

SOL: (*Offstage.*) I'll bring it out, Oscar.

SOL enters and sees ALICE.

RENA: Sol, this is –

SOL goes over to ALICE and offers his hand.

SOL: Sol Walker. (*Suspiciously.*) And you've met Rena.

ALICE: Yes, we were discussing the Olympics. Rena and myself.

SOL: 'Rena and I.'

ALICE: Sorry?

SOL: Sorry. It's 'Rena and I', not 'Rena and myself'.

ALICE: Thank you.

SOL: Sorry. (*Beat.*) You are early.

ALICE and RENA overlap.

ALICE: I like to be early.

RENA: She likes to be early.

SOL: Yes, well I wasn't expecting anyone until next month. That is what the university said. (*Beat.*) Sorry for the mess.

RENA: (*Whispers.*) She also likes to be neat.

SOL: Thank you, Rena.

SOL picks up the books that ALICE brought with her.

ALICE: What do you think of Isegawa? *Abyssinian Chronicles* is –

SOL: I haven't read it. Yet.

ALICE: What about Okot p'Bitek? You must have read *Song of Lawino*.

Beat.

SOL: Again, not yet.

ALICE: What do you think of Grace Ogot? Her writings are for me, phenomenal.

SOL: I'm not – she's not a writer that I am familiar with.

ALICE: Mary Karooro Okurut?

SOL laughs uncomfortably.

Have you read any East African writers?

SOL: Well I have read *Things Fall Apart.* Some of it. Most of it.
/ Not that Achebe's East African.

ALICE: Achebe's Nigerian.

SOL: / That's what I was saying.

ALICE: Nigeria's in West Africa.

SOL: I know that.

ALICE: Everyone has read *Things Fall Apart.*

SOL: Of course, but...

ALICE: (*To RENA.*) What authors do you like?

SOL: I was thinking we could start with –

ALICE: Rena.

RENA: What?

ALICE: What authors do you like?

RENA: Authors?

ALICE: It would be great to discuss with you the writers that
we enjoy.

RENA: You what?

RENA breaks into laughter.

ALICE:

RENA stops laughing. Pause.

RENA:

ALICE:

Beat.

RENA: I'm…I'm not really a reader.

ALICE: Oh. (*Beat.*) Neither was I for a long time. For a long time I did not see a book.

ALICE caresses the pile of books that she brought.

RENA: Maybe I should find Oscar.

RENA goes to exit the schoolhouse.

ALICE: Wait.

ALICE looks at the pile of books, selects one and holds it out to RENA. RENA hesitates before taking the book as she walks out of the schoolhouse. ALICE makes the slightest move to follow her, but is stopped by SOL's voice.

SOL: Well I suppose we should get started.

SOL picks up ALICE's books as ALICE looks around the building.

I apologise for earlier; I should know all these writers. I just haven't had a chance to properly prepare. I was in Cambodia just before, then had to go home for personal reasons and time just slipped away from me. I must get to reading, then, mustn't I? I didn't realise someone was coming today. Not that it's your fault. The university wasn't sending anyone until we got the building ready. That is what they said.

SOL looks at ALICE, who shrugs.

ALICE: I do not know what they have said.

SOL: Is there a lot of red tape and bureaucracy? Usually is with institutions. They don't know how to communicate, do they? It's all paperwork and more paperwork. I can't imagine the university being any different.

ALICE: I do not know. I have never been to the university.

Beat.

SOL: But you have been recruited through the university.

ALICE shakes her head.

ALICE: No.

SOL: Yes, you are one of the teachers I am here to train.

Pause. ALICE realises that she hasn't introduced herself. She holds out her hand.

ALICE: Alice Kwagala.

SOL:

ALICE: I am to be one of your students.

SOL: You're a…

ALICE: Was. Soldier. Yes.

SOL: Oh. Sorry, it was the books.

ALICE: What? Is something wrong with my books?

SOL: No, I just didn't expect you, the students to be…I mean. Welcome, Alice.

SOL finally takes ALICE's hand. Beat.

ALICE: Thank you.

SCENE 3

The schoolhouse is starting to take shape. A few posters – of White Western authors – and learning charts decorate the walls. There are two rough, newly made benches in the corner.

RENA sits on one of the benches, reading the book ALICE gave her, Song of Lawino. *She reads a passage that she finds amusing, so reads it aloud.*

RENA: 'Ocol says he is a modern man,

A progressive and civilised man,
He says he has read extensively and widely,
And he can no longer live with a thing like me
Who cannot distinguish between good and bad.'

RENA laughs at what she's just read. She sarcastically repeats the last two lines.

'And he can no longer live with a thing like me
Who cannot distinguish between good and bad.'

She laughs again, but there is a slight discomfort in it. RENA continues to read to herself.

She comes across a passage in the poem that makes her uncomfortable. Long pause as RENA turns what she has just read over in her head. She finally reads the passage aloud.

'He says I am blocking his progress,
My head, he says,
Is as big as that of an elephant
But it is only bones,
There is no brain in it,
He says that I am only wasting his time.'

RENA closes her eyes, trying to make sense of her feelings about what she has just read. She decides to recite the last passage again. RENA starts to play around with the rhythm of the passage; starting, stopping and starting again, giving it her distinct flavour.

As RENA delivers her version of the text, OSCAR enters, carrying a new bench. RENA continues to recite aloud, oblivious to OSCAR's presence. OSCAR puts the bench down quietly and sits, listening to RENA. When RENA finishes, OSCAR applauds.

OSCAR: Encore, encore!

RENA is startled.

RENA: What you doing, creeping round corners like that, man?!

OSCAR: Sorry. I didn't want to disrupt your flow. Which was brilliant, by the way.

RENA quickly closes the book.

RENA: Fuck off, Oscar.

OSCAR: What? That was. It was lovely.

RENA: Yeah, yeah, take the piss.

RENA puts the book out of sight.

OSCAR: Must be good.

RENA: What?

OSCAR: The book. To have you reciting from it.

RENA: Not really, no. (*Beat.*) A bit dry, actually.

Pause.

OSCAR: That's a shame.

RENA: Why?

OSCAR: I was hoping you could pass it over when you were done. I need a good read.

RENA looks at OSCAR sceptically, but he's examining the bench. Beat.

RENA: Is Alice – is she coming? Today I mean.

OSCAR: I don't see why she should, but you could ask Sol.

RENA: No thanks.

OSCAR: She seems alright, doesn't she?

RENA shrugs. OSCAR smiles.

Must be nice to have another girl here, huh?

RENA: Alice isn't really a girl, is she though?

OSCAR: Pardon?

RENA: What I mean is, she's not young.

OSCAR: Seventeen; same as you.

RENA: Yeah, but she ain't like normal seventeen year-olds. Coz for one, she's all clever, man. None of my spars have never seen these many books, let alone read them. And she's not even at uni. That ain't normal. Not for seventeen. She even looks old.

OSCAR: And what's old?

RENA: Twenty-five, twenty-six.

OSCAR whistles.

OSCAR: Ancient.

RENA: She does though, right?

OSCAR: I guess she does, yeah, if twenty-five is old.

RENA: It is where I'm from.

OSCAR: What does that make me, then? If twenty-five is old?

RENA: Really old.

OSCAR laughs.

If war adds ten years, no thank you.

OSCAR: I don't think premature ageing was the occupational hazard they were majorly concerned with.

RENA: The stuff she must have done; that definitely ain't normal. And don't ask 'what's normal'. You know what I mean.

OSCAR: But maybe your normal and her normal are two different things.

RENA: My normal is that I ain't never been made to kill nobody.

OSCAR: No, but you have chosen to beat the shit out of some Somali kids.

RENA:

OSCAR:

RENA: That was…

OSCAR: Different? Yes, it was.

> *Pause.*

RENA: I know you don't agree with me – you don't have to.

OSCAR: You're right there, Rena; I don't.

RENA: So –

OSCAR: But I don't have to give up hope, either. Not on anyone. Even though I'm getting too old for this shit. Building benches in foreign lands is taking its toll.

> *Pause.*

RENA: That's why you do this, then.

OSCAR: Do what? Make benches?

RENA: 'In foreign lands.' It's White man's guilt, ain't it?

OSCAR: You don't hold back, do you?

RENA: Or do you have a Jesus complex; with all this carpentry and shit?

OSCAR: I'm an atheist.

RENA: And I'm wheat intolerant, but I'll still scoff down slices of ginger cake. (*Beat.*) I'd kill for some ginger cake right now.

> *Beat.*

OSCAR: No, I don't have White man's guilt. And I don't like to think I've got a Jesus complex.

RENA: But you don't know for sure.

OSCAR: What do we know for sure? Actually?

RENA: Well I definitely know you wouldn't catch me out here working for nothing.

OSCAR: But you are out here.

RENA: Normally, I mean. Normally I wouldn't be.

OSCAR: That word 'normal' again. If the world was 'normal', none of us would have to be here, working for 'nothing.' People wouldn't have been placed in the situation where we need to do this.

RENA: You and Sol, you're so right on, aren't you? Fair-trade this; freedom of speech that. Always 'doing good'.

OSCAR shrugs.

OSCAR: Could do 'bad', but it doesn't suit my complexion. (*Beat.*) I have no problem standing up for what's right.

RENA: And it's all coz you want to make the world a better place, yeah?

OSCAR: No. No, it's more selfish than that. (*Pause.*) I don't want to be the wanker that did nothing. And I've been there before. I've been that wanker, the one that stood there and did nothing and it's the most revolting place to be.

Briefly, OSCAR remembers the shameful moment. Then he shakes it off.

So I decided never to do nothing again.

RENA: Yeah, but you don't have to be knocking out benches in Africa.

OSCAR: That's because I choose to.

RENA: You've got money. Why don't you –

OSCAR: And how do you know?

RENA: Come on now, Oscar. I can smell the posh coming right off you. Even covered in sawdust.

OSCAR laughs.

OSCAR: Okay, my family's got money.

RENA: So you're minted. Just write a cheque. I know I would.

OSCAR: I've done that too. And I felt a complete tit.

RENA: A wanker and a tit.

OSCAR: Yes, a wanker and a tit. And what I learned was that writing a cheque is easy, Rena. Rather get splinters in my hands than ink on my fingers.

Beat. RENA bursts out laughing. SOL enters carrying a folder full of paperwork.

RENA: (*To SOL.*) Someone who might possibly be more of a wanker than you, bruv.

SOL: Rena!

OSCAR: That's alright, Youngblood. At least I know I'm a wanker.

RENA: Me and Oscar –

SOL: Oscar and I –

RENA: – were just having a chat.

SOL: Talking isn't what we are here to do. (*To OSCAR.*) Don't let her skive off, Oscar.

OSCAR: Lil' Sis was just wanting to know if the lovely Alice was joining us today.

SOL: (*To RENA.*) Why?!

RENA: No reason.

OSCAR: I think it's good there's another female about. All this manliness can become overwhelming, I know.

OSCAR flexes his muscles.

RENA: Whatever. (*To SOL.*) I just wanted to ask her about something.

SOL: What?

RENA: None of your business.

SOL: Don't go upsetting her, alright?

RENA: Upset her how?

SOL: She's had enough upset in one lifetime.

RENA: So what could I possibly do that's worse than what she's been through?

SOL: You'd think of something, I'm sure.

RENA: Cheers.

SOL: I'm serious, Rena.

RENA: And I'm –

OSCAR: (*To RENA.*) Wait. Cool it.

RENA: Me? He's always assuming that I'm up to something.

OSCAR: (*To RENA.*) Keep it calm.

SOL: (*To RENA.*) I know you.

RENA: Wait 'til I assume my foot up your arse.

OSCAR: Youngblood, I don't think that Lil' Sis here would do anything intentional to hurt Alice. (*To RENA.*) Right?

SOL: I'm just saying to be gentle with Alice.

RENA: Me be gentle?! She's the one's put bullets through people's heads, man. She should be gentle with me.

Silence.

SOL: You never disappoint, do you Rena?

RENA: What? It's the truth.

SOL: And you wonder why people always think you're up to something; it's because you are always up to something!

RENA: Why should I lie coz you don't want to hurt her feelings? Poor little Alice's feelings. It's coz you fancy her, don't you?

SOL: You know what, just stop talking. Be quiet and go back to work – or start working, whatever it is that you were doing before you opened your mouth. Better still, do whatever Oscar tells you to do.

OSCAR: I don't –

SOL: You know, you can tell her to do whatever you need, Oscar. She's here to work.

RENA: Ah, excuse me!

SOL: You're here to work, Rena.

RENA bows her head in mock subservience.

RENA: Yessir, Master Sol.

SOL: Oh, stop it, Rena. Just help Oscar, okay?

RENA: Me do whatever Master Sol say do.

SOL: Please!

RENA: That's what ol' Rena here aim to do – me aim to please. (*To OSCAR.*) Wanna have a look at me?

RENA hops up on one of the benches.

Me got good teeth. And birthing hips too, Master Oscar. I can birth you a whole mess of pickney. Come and have a good look, Master Oscar.

SOL: / Stop this minstrel show! Now!

RENA: Do I hear five? No? Come on, five pounds. No, it wouldn't have been pounds, would it? Would it, back then? / Me so stupid.

SOL: Do you know how ignorant you sound?!

RENA: Anyway, Going once, going twice, sold! (*Points to OSCAR.*) To the gentleman in the –

SOL yanks RENA down from the bench.

SOL: Shut the fuck up and play the nigger in your own time.

SOL immediately regrets saying 'nigger' in front of OSCAR.

RENA: Who's playing?

RENA has clocked SOL's embarrassment and laughs.

SOL: Get on with sorting this out.

SOL shoves the folder into RENA's hands. She lets the folder fall to the floor. Papers scatter everywhere.

RENA:

SOL:

RENA: And here was me thinking the Empire had left Africa.

RENA exits. Silence. SOL bends down to collect the scattered paperwork. OSCAR bends down to help him.

SOL: No, that's okay, I've got it Oscar.

OSCAR: Youngblood –

SOL: I can't believe she did that. Sorry, Oscar. I don't know what to say really. She really does my head in, you know. Still –

OSCAR: Sol...

SOL avoids looking OSCAR in the eye.

SOL: I better get on with this. If I don't, Kate's going to have my guts for garters. She's been after me since we got here to get this sorted. Should have had it done before I left London.

Silence. The men continue to collect the paper from the floor. ALICE enters with two armloads of books and posters. OSCAR rushes to take some of the books off her.

ALICE: How are you all? Well, I hope.

OSCAR: You rob a printing press, Alice?

ALICE: Give thanks to the Christian charity.

OSCAR: (*Sarcastically.*) Praise be.

RENA enters carrying another stack of books. OSCAR gestures for SOL to help RENA with the books she's carrying. Beat. SOL offers RENA his help, but she turns away from him. RENA plops the books down.

ALICE: (*To RENA.*) Thank you. (*To SOL.*) I hope they meet with your approval, teacher.

SOL comes over to inspect the books.

SOL: (*To ALICE.*) You'll be happy to know that I've just finished *Abyssinian Chronicles.*

ALICE: Yes?

SOL: Very good. I like it a lot.

ALICE: I knew you would.

SOL: Read it all in one go.

Pause as SOL waits for ALICE to respond.

ALICE: Yes?

SOL: Nothing.

RENA: (*To ALICE.*) He wants you to give him a pat on the head. (*Beat.*) I've held a gun.

SOL: Rena!

RENA: Twice.

SOL: I'm going to kill her.

RENA: Two guns, actually.

ALICE picks up the book that she gave RENA.

ALICE: Are you enjoying this?

RENA: The first was nothing much, not like what you probably used.

ALICE: I hope you are enjoying it.

RENA: A replica what got converted. Nice little number. The other was shite; a popgun toy, basically.

ALICE: It is my favourite poem.

RENA: I didn't fire them or nothing. Not at no one.

ALICE: Do you want me to congratulate you?

SOL chuckles to himself.

RENA: No, I –

ALICE: What then?

RENA: I just thought you'd like to know that we had something in common.

ALICE: It could be called our national poem.

RENA: That we aren't that different, you and me.

ALICE: P'Bitek could be called our national poet.

RENA: That I don't mind that you're a bit gangsta. That's alright by me.

ALICE: Let me know when you have finished it.

RENA: I –

ALICE cuts RENA a look. Silence.

SOL: It is hard to believe that you two are the same age.

ALICE: Rena and m – Rena and I?

SOL: Yes. She seems so young, doesn't she?

ALICE: And I do not?

SOL: Well you seem… You are less like a baby.

ALICE: I am not a baby.

SOL: I know.

ALICE: Rena is not a baby either.

SOL: No, but she is immature.

RENA: Fuck off, Sol.

SOL makes a face that says, 'I told you so.'

OSCAR: Are you like this with your brothers and sisters?

ALICE: I do not have brothers and sisters.

RENA: Man, I'd love to be the only child.

SOL: (*To RENA.*) You and me both.

RENA: Eh, eh; you and I.

Beat. If looks could kill…

ALICE: My family are dead.

OSCAR: What? Everyone?

ALICE: (*To RENA.*) Yes. Everyone.

OSCAR: Shit.

SOL: I'm really sorry.

ALICE: Do not be sorry. I do not want your sorry.

SOL: Sor –

ALICE: I do not want your sorry.

   SOL nods.

SOL: I admire you.

ALICE: (*Sarcastically.*) Sorry and admiration.

SOL: I didn't mean it that –

ALICE: Why?

SOL: Why?

ALICE: Yes.

SOL: Why I admire you? (*Beat.*) Well, because…

ALICE: Because what? Why your admiration?

SOL: Because of your history, I mean.

ALICE: Oh.

SOL: Because even though you are a victim of a corrupt –

ALICE: A survivor.

SOL: Sorry?

ALICE: I am survivor.

SOL: Of course, but what I mean is –

ALICE: Am I dead?

SOL: Sorry?

ALICE: Again, 'sorry'. Am I dead?

SOL: No, but –

ALICE: Then I am a survivor.

OSCAR: Yes, you are, Alice.

SOL: Yes, of course you are, yes. But do you not think –

OSCAR: Youngblood…

SOL: Do you not think that the Ugandan government and the rebel army both have responsibility for what they have allowed to happen?

OSCAR: Of course they do. And so does –

SOL: The systematic abuses of human rights; abducting and recruiting children to fight. Brutalising and displacing the civilian population through rape, murder, looting.

OSCAR: Yes, but –

SOL: Breaking ceasefires. Don't they have to be held accountable?

OSCAR: And so does the international community for turning a blind eye. We all have –

ALICE: But me? I am responsible for me, now.

SOL: You didn't ask to be in that situation. Sometimes there are situations that you find yourself in.

ALICE: Or maybe there are situations that you choose to be in.

SOL: What does that mean? What, are you saying that you knew what you were doing?

ALICE: Why not?

SOL: You didn't choose to be soldiers.

ALICE: I did.

Silence.

Not everyone. Not most of us. But I did. All of your students will be survivors, Sol. Whether they chose to fight or not.

Silence. ALICE sees the posters on the wall.

What we need are some Ugandan writers on the wall. Ugandan students see the faces of their own writers.

ALICE hands SOL the posters that she has brought with her.

SOL: Thanks.

Pause. SOL realises that ALICE is waiting for him to put the posters on the wall. He grabs some tape and begins to hang the posters. OSCAR helps him out.

OSCAR: Let me give you a hand, Youngblood.

ALICE: (*To SOL.*) Have you read any of the other books that I brought? Except for *Abyssinian Chronicles*.

SOL: Not yet.

ALICE: Though you have read *Things Fall Apart* of course.

SOL: That's –

ALICE: Well, 'most of it'.

SOL: That's not –

OSCAR laughs.

OSCAR: Even I've read *Things Fall Apart*. All of it.

ALICE laughs.

SOL: Thank you –

OSCAR: All of it.

SOL: Thank you, Oscar.

ALICE laughs even harder.

OSCAR: Good book, that. Anyway, Achebe's Nigerian.

SOL: Yes, we know, Oscar.

OSCAR: Nigeria's in West Africa.

Now ALICE is almost in tears with laughter.

SOL:

OSCAR: Oh, come on. We're just winding you up, Youngblood.

OSCAR pats SOL on the back as he exits the school. Beat.

SOL: In Cambodia they liked the writers I taught.

ALICE: I am glad they did. I am sure they would have liked Okot p'Bitek as well.

Beat.

SOL: I'm sure they would've.

ALICE: Good. Shall we have a look at *Song of Lawino*? Your other students will be expecting to study it.

Beat.

SOL: Of course.

OSCAR: (*Offstage.*) Youngblood, can you give me a quick hand, please?

SOL: Be right back.

SOL exits. ALICE looks after him. Pause.

ALICE: I think he is a fraud.

RENA: Who, Sol?

ALICE nods.

ALICE: He is like so many that come here to 'help'. They want Africans to be victims.

RENA: What do you mean?

ALICE: He wants to help us on his terms. With his books and his culture.

RENA: But he's been doing this shit for years; volunteering abroad, I mean. Charity work. Since he was my age.

ALICE: Our age. You were right. He does want a pat on the head. (*Beat.*) Sorry to talk so unkindly about your brother.

RENA: I do it all the time. (*Beat.*) Not many people do, though. I thought everybody out here would think the sun shines out of his backside.

ALICE: Why?

RENA: Why? Coz…I don't know. Coz he's helping people. He's helping save the world. (*Beat.*) Isn't he?

ALICE shrugs.

ALICE: What do you think of him?

RENA: Me?

ALICE nods. RENA shrugs.

I don't know. He's my brother, innit?

ALICE laughs.

ALICE: Innit?

RENA: Yeah, innit.

ALICE laughs again.

What?

ALICE: Innit.

RENA: At least Sol, he means well. Not like me. People, they think I –

ALICE: What do you think of yourself?

RENA: Me?

ALICE:

RENA:

> (*Pauses.*) I'm just Rena, innit?

> *ALICE laughs.*

ALICE: Innit.

RENA: Innit.

> *SOL pops his head around the door to see the girls laughing.*

SCENE 4

The schoolhouse.

The school is really coming together. There are more benches and now a few desks as well. ALICE and RENA are alone; RENA is sanding down a rather wonky bench while ALICE is absorbed in a notebook. On the floor between them is a melted and misshapen king-size KitKat.

RENA: I almost forgot I had that. (*Beat.*) Stocked up, didn't I? Didn't know what to expect. Didn't know if you had chocolate out here. Can't live without –

ALICE: Shh.

RENA: Sorry.

> *ALICE goes back to reading from the notebook. RENA runs her hand along the bench. She looks at the other benches.*

> Oscar's a good carpenter. I think he should –

ALICE: Quiet!

ALICE closes the notebook.

RENA:

ALICE:

Beat.

RENA: Rubbish, ain't it?

ALICE points to the posters on the wall.

ALICE: One day, we will put your picture up on a wall.

RENA: Stop chatting shit.

RENA reaches for the notebook, but ALICE holds it out of her reach.

ALICE: I am not chatting shit; I mean it. Your books will sell on the internet and you will give lectures at universities and I will brag and be the big show-off, 'This is my friend, don't you know?' 'Yes, I am friends with Rena Walker, don't you know?' You will be invited on Oprah's Book Club and I will go to America and sit in the audience with your mother and father and Oprah will ask me questions and I will say, 'Rena dedicated her first book to me, don't you know?' 'I always knew that she would be a success, don't you know?'

RENA: 'Don't you know?'!

ALICE: 'Don't you know?'!

RENA laughs.

RENA: 'Don't you know?'

They both laugh.

ALICE: Which is your mother's favourite story?

RENA: She doesn't have one.

ALICE: She must have one. They are all so different. They are all very good and different, which is very nice.

ALICE looks at RENA for a response. RENA shakes her head.

RENA: She doesn't have one.

ALICE nods, thinking she understands.

ALICE: She likes them all. They are all her favourites. A mother would not have favourites.

RENA: No. (*Beat.*) No, Alice.

ALICE: You could tell them that now you are a writer. You could send them your writings.

RENA: They don't want to hear from me.

Pause.

ALICE: We will send them your writings. We will type everything and email it to them.

RENA: My parents aren't that wired up. They've only got one mobile between them.

ALICE: That is primitive. Nothing would get done in Uganda if we didn't have mobile phones. (*Beat.*) We can go to the city and post your writings to your mother and father. Yes?

RENA shrugs her shoulders.

Yes.

ALICE toasts their decision with a piece of chocolate.

Julius would have liked this. I always shared my treasures with him.

RENA: Julius? Was that your boyfriend or something?

ALICE: No.

RENA nudges ALICE.

RENA: What, was he someone you fancied, then?

ALICE: No.

Beat.

RENA: I was hoping the blokes out here would be fit.
Somebody I could fancy, you know. Go on the pull. (*Beat.*)
You ever had sex?

ALICE: I have never had a boyfriend.

RENA: You mean you ain't never –

OSCAR enters.

OSCAR: Is that chocolate?

RENA offers him some.

RENA: My emergency stash.

OSCAR: Excellent.

OSCAR breaks off a piece and shoves it into his mouth. OSCAR rolls around in delight.

Ohh, how great is that?

The girls laugh at him.

RENA: 'Don't you know?'!

ALICE: 'Don't you know?'!

The girls laugh even louder. OSCAR shoves more chocolate into his mouth.

OSCAR: What's that?

ALICE: Rena was just –

RENA: Alice, quiet, man!

RENA tries to cover ALICE's mouth, but ALICE pushes her away. ALICE holds up RENA's notebook.

ALICE: Rena let me read a collection of her work. She's an author of world-class fiction.

RENA: Shut up!

ALICE: World-class, Oscar. And when she is famous, I will say, 'Rena Walker, oh yes, I discovered her in Uganda, don't you know.'

OSCAR laughs.

RENA: 'Don't you know?'!

ALICE: 'Don't you know?'!

OSCAR: Oh yeah? Well, I overheard her reciting from memory that *Song of Lawino*.

RENA: Oscar!

OSCAR: Absolutely beautiful.

ALICE looks at RENA, who is blushing.

ALICE: You memorised the poem?

RENA shrugs.

RENA: Not all of it. Just the first bits. (*Beat.*) It's a long poem.

ALICE:

RENA: What?

ALICE:

Pause.

RENA: What, it's a good poem, man.

Beat.

ALICE: World-class, Oscar.

OSCAR: 'Don't you know?'!

The girls laugh. SOL enters.

RENA: 'Don't you know?'!

ALICE: 'Don't you know?'!

OSCAR: 'Don't you know?'!

RENA, ALICE and OSCAR laugh. SOL joins in, though he's not sure what he's laughing at.

SOL: What's that?

RENA: 'Don't you know?'!

SOL: What?

ALICE: 'Don't you know?'!

SOL: What is it?

OSCAR: Youngblood, we're just messing about.

RENA: 'Don't you know?'!

SOL: What's the joke?

OSCAR: Nothing. It's nothing; something silly.

The laughter dies down, but there are titters every now and then. SOL looks disappointed.

SOL: Oscar, Kate wants to know if you can have a look at that door in the dorm.

ALICE: (*Whispers.*) 'Don't you know?'

RENA tries but fails to suppress a giggle. She offers him some of the chocolate.

RENA: You want some chocolate?

SOL reaches for the chocolate, but then sees the wrapper.

SOL: I can't eat that.

ALICE: Don't you like chocolate?

RENA: Why? It's not gone off.

OSCAR: Oh Youngblood, you've got to have some.

SOL: Oscar, you shouldn't be eating that either.

OSCAR: Why, what's wrong with it?

SOL: It's…

OSCAR: Poisoned?

OSCAR grabs at his throat and pretends to be dying from being poisoned.

Rena…Alice…

OSCAR 'dies'. The girls laugh.

SOL: It's a KitKat.

RENA: (*To OSCAR.*) Stupid, you are.

OSCAR 'rises from the dead'.

SOL: It's made by Nestlé.

OSCAR: Oh, Youngblood…

SOL: Nestlé, Oscar. With their track record.

RENA: What's the matter with Nestlé? Like Cadbury tastes any better.

SOL: Do you know what Nestlé has done to the developing world?

RENA: Here we go. Does everything have to be a sermon, man?

SOL: All the pollution? Privatisation of water?

RENA: It's just chocolate.

OSCAR: I know all that.

SOL: They aggressively encourage mothers to use their formula instead of breastfeeding.

OSCAR: So don't teach your grandmother to suck eggs.

SOL: So what you doing with that in your mouth?

RENA: It's just choc –

OSCAR: Because sometimes Youngblood, a KitKat is just a KitKat. Sometimes I just want a KitKat to be a fucking KitKat. We can't save the world all the time.

SOL looks from OSCAR to RENA in disgust, as if to blame RENA for OSCAR's comment.

RENA: What?!

ALICE: I like it.

SOL: You've got to be kidding, right. Surely you know what companies like that have done to the Third World and –

RENA: Come on, Alice. Let's finish this outside.

RENA and ALICE exit.

OSCAR: What is it, Youngblood?

SOL: Nothing.

OSCAR: Oh, come on.

SOL: I've just got things to get on with and I can't do them with people in the way.

OSCAR: No, there's more to it than that.

Pause.

SOL: It's Mum.

OSCAR: Not bad news, is it? She's not gotten worse?

SOL: No. She's fine.

OSCAR: What then?

Beat.

SOL: She would send me fair-trade chocolate. And her ginger cake. In care packages. She would send me care packages, wherever I was.

OSCAR: I remember that ginger cake.

SOL: She makes a good ginger cake, my mum.

OSCAR:

OSCAR pats SOL on the back. RENA returns.

RENA: Forgot my notebook.

SOL exits. RENA and OSCAR exchange a look.

OSCAR: He's right, you know. We shouldn't be eating Nestlé products. But I bloody well love KitKats. (*Beat.*) Back to work.

OSCAR exits. RENA picks up her notebook, flicking through the pages. UNCLE YUSEFU enters.

YUSEFU: Good morning, my sister.

Beat.

RENA: He just left.

YUSEFU: He who?

RENA: You're looking for Sol, yeah? Well he just –

YUSEFU: No, I am not.

RENA: Oh.

RENA offers him her hand.

Sorry. I'm Rena.

They shake. RENA continues to hold his hand long after the handshake has finished. UNCLE YUSEFU smiles.

YUSEFU: Ah, you know of our custom.

RENA: A friend taught me.

YUSEFU: It is good to see that our Western friends are embracing Ugandan customs. Are you enjoying my country?

RENA: I think it's a bit alright, actually. (*Beat.*) You want me to show you round our school?

YUSEFU: Please.

RENA: Well, these are some of the books that we've got. Most are donations, but –

UNCLE YUSEFU picks up the book ALICE gave RENA.

YUSEFU: *Song of Lawino.*

RENA: Good, right?

YUSEFU: You have read *Song of Lawino*?!

RENA: Of course, man.

UNCLE YUSEFU laughs.

See, we got the author's picture on the wall and everything. And these are the benches and desks that Oscar made.

UNCLE YUSEFU admires the benches. RENA points to the bench that she and ALICE were working on earlier.

Me and Alice made this one. Nice, right? If a bit wonky.

He moves over to it.

YUSEFU: Alice Kwagala?

RENA: Yeah. How do you know, Alice?

Before he can answer, ALICE and OSCAR enter, laughing and repeating 'Don't you know?'. ALICE stops short when she sees UNCLE YUSEFU.

YUSEFU: Ah, I was just about to tell your friend Rena that I have not seen my favourite niece in such a long time. I have not seen you since you were so tall: (*He indicates the height with his hand.*) You have grown. And your friend – Rena – and Rena has told me you have taught her our ways. I am so glad you have not lost our ways. And that you have passed them on to your Western friends. Never forget them. Never. Is she not beautiful? Is my niece not beautiful. The very image of my sister. Your mother sends you her love. (*Beat.*) Come, give your favourite uncle a kiss.

He goes to embrace her.

RENA: You what? Uncle?

YUSEFU: Yes, her Uncle Yusefu.

RENA: This Alice Kwagala?

YUSEFU: This Alice Kwagala.

Beat.

RENA: Nah, mate. Alice, she ain't got no uncle. She ain't got –

YUSEFU: She has me.

RENA: But Alice told us…

YUSEFU: Yes, what did Alice tell you?

RENA: She said – (*To ALICE.*) You said –

UNCLE YUSEFU nods his understanding.

YUSEFU: I suppose she did not speak of me. You children always forget your elders. I have not seen her for such a long time. Yes, my sister is very proud of her only daughter.

RENA:

ALICE:

YUSEFU: She wishes that she could see you, but she knows that you are doing well. They insist that you must visit them soon. (*Beat.*) It does the eyes of this old man good to see you so well.

Beat. RENA goes to leave.

ALICE: Rena….

RENA: 'Niece' Alice.

RENA pushes past ALICE.

YUSEFU: Your friend is upset.

ALICE pulls away from UNCLE YUSEFU. He notices that OSCAR has seen this, so shrugs, then offers his hand.

Yusefu Nakabiri.

OSCAR: Oscar Parsons. (*Beat.*) Rena must've gotten the wrong end of the stick. Alice?

ALICE:

OSCAR:

YUSEFU: I hope that she will be okay.

OSCAR: Are you okay, Alice?

YUSEFU: She will be fine. It must be a surprise to see my face.

OSCAR: Alice?

Beat. OSCAR studies ALICE. ALICE nods.

YUSEFU: See? Her uncle is here now?

ALICE: Oscar, please see if Rena is okay.

OSCAR: Are you –

ALICE: Thank you.

Beat.

OSCAR: Okay.

OSCAR exits.

YUSEFU: They seem very friendly. I am glad that you / are with friendly people.

ALICE: Why are you here?! I have done nothing!

YUSEFU: That is not true, is it, Alice?

ALICE:

YUSEFU:

ALICE: Why do you not leave me alone? Please!

Silence.

Please?

YUSEFU: No. Why should you find peace?

SCENE 5

A few hours later.

UNCLE YUSEFU holds court.

YUSEFU: Alice was a lovely child, lovely and forever laughing. She was a much loved child. She gets that from her mother, my sister. My youngest sister.

SOL: Do you have a large family?

YUSEFU: Oh yes. Many sisters and brothers who have had many children and grandchildren. There have been many additions to the family since Alice went away. (*To ALICE.*) You have many new nephews and one niece. Your mother is a happy grandmother. Very happy, yes.

ALICE:

YUSEFU:

Beat.

SOL: It is understandable why Alice lied about not having a family. The shame must be overwhelming.

OSCAR shoots SOL a look which SOL doesn't see.

OSCAR: It must have been hard.

YUSEFU: What?

OSCAR: Losing Alice to the war.

Beat.

YUSEFU: Yes. We thought she was lost for ever.

UNCLE YUSEFU puts his arm around ALICE, who visibly tenses up.

RENA: (*Mutters.*) She should've been.

YUSEFU: Many children were. Many, many. Yes, it was hard. But now I have found her.

OSCAR: It must be a relief.

YUSEFU: Indeed. She should not have stayed away. It was very selfish. We are your family. (*Beat.*) Yes, very selfish.

OSCAR: Maybe she was trying to protect you.

YUSEFU: Protection?

OSCAR: From reprisals. Maybe Alice didn't want the village turning on you. It often happens if a child soldier tries to return home.

YUSEFU: Does it?

OSCAR:

UNCLE YUSEFU picks up the volume of William Blake's poetry that SOL has been reading.

William Blake.

UNCLE YUSEFU nods approvingly.

SOL: Do you –

YUSEFU: (*Reciting from memory.*)
    'Tiger, tiger, burning bright
    In the forests of the night,
    What immortal hand or eye
    Could frame thy fearful symmetry?'

SOL stares in awe; it is clear that UNCLE YUSEFU is waiting for acknowledgment of his recitation. SOL applauds the hammy performance, in reply to which UNCLE YUSEFU shrugs in false modesty. He launches back into the poem.

    'In what distant deeps or skies
    Burnt the fire of thine eyes?'

He takes a dramatic breath.

    'On what wings – '

SOL: You do know your poetry.

YUSEFU: No, no, only a few pieces here, a few there. Those that I have been taught. An English gentleman from long ago. Before independence.

SOL: You know Blake, Alice knows Ugandan literature; what am I doing here?

SOL laughs with just a touch of self-pity, just a touch of bitterness.

YUSEFU: No, Sol. We need you. I am not so clever like you, Sol. I am sure you know much wonderful English literature.

SOL: I was thinking that maybe I should base the curriculum around Ugandan writers.

UNCLE YUSEFU shakes his head.

YUSEFU: No. Eliot, Tennyson, Shakespeare. Shakespeare; 'Once more unto the breach, dear friends, once more'; ah, that is what we want! Kipling, Blake. We want our children to learn the Queen's English.

OSCAR: The Queen's English?! The Empire doesn't own you anymore. What of this country's literary heritage? Some brilliant writing –

YUSEFU: The world does not take these writers seriously. Do they? Who has heard of Okot p'Bitek? Moses Isegawa? Hmm?

OSCAR: But that isn't –

YUSEFU: But that is the point. In all honesty, had you heard of Isegawa before you stepped off the plane in Kampala? Grace Ogot? Mary Karooro Okurut?

OSCAR:

YUSEFU: Before Alice brought these books before you, had you heard the names Richard Ntiru or Robert Serumaga? I could go on.

He points to the posters on the wall.

My niece, she has made a noble effort, but let's be honest, yes? These writers, I am sure, will not be remembered by history. They are African writers. African. And history has never been kind to our lot.

Pause.

SOL: It was Alice who suggested Isegawa. From the beginning I wanted T S Eliot.

YUSEFU: And that is why you are the teacher.

SOL smiles.

SOL: Let me show you my favourite passage in *The Wasteland.*

As SOL and UNCLE YUSEFU look through the volume of poetry, they bump into RENA.

RENA: Fucking watch it!

SOL: Rena!

ALICE goes to RENA.

ALICE: Rena…

RENA pointedly walks past ALICE.

SOL: Don't worry about her. (*To RENA.*) Rena is a selfish brat.

RENA lashes out and knocks a stack of books over as she storms out of the schoolhouse.

See?

YUSEFU: Yes, children no longer respect their elders.

Silence. OSCAR goes to ALICE and puts his arm around her.

OSCAR: She'll come round.

ALICE: She will not. I would not if I were her.

OSCAR: She's just surprised, that's all.

ALICE shrugs OSCAR's arm from her shoulders. She goes to collect the books that RENA knocked over.

ALICE: You think I am not to be trusted as well.

OSCAR: I think you had your reasons.

SOL: Oscar, we better get going. (*To YUSEFU.*) We're heading to the city. Please, make yourself at home.

OSCAR starts to escort ALICE out of the school.

YUSEFU: Alice, please stay with your old Uncle Yusefu and read poetry.

ALICE stops where she stands.

OSCAR: You sure?

Silence from ALICE.

YUSEFU: Please, let an old man be read to by his long-lost niece.

SOL forces the book of poetry in her hands.

SOL: See you in a bit.

SOL exits.

OSCAR: Alice?

ALICE:

YUSEFU:

Beat.

ALICE: Please go.

OSCAR tries to catch ALICE's eye, but she avoids his gaze. He exits. UNCLE YUSEFU takes a step closer to ALICE when SOL pops his head around the corner.

SOL: I have some Wordsworth in one of my boxes. I'll root it out for you later.

UNCLE YUSEFU smiles his thanks then sees SOL off with a wave. SOL exits. Beat.

YUSEFU: For that one, I will play the savage; he likes it. 'You do know your poetry.' He is a... (*Searches for the word.*) ...tosser.

He laughs at the word. Silence.

ALICE: Please go.

YUSEFU: Oscar, he is interesting.

He caresses one of the benches.

Beautiful craftsmanship. Almost as good as my father. Rena is very pretty.

ALICE shoots him a look then realises that she has risen to the bait.

Very pretty. But now she is very sad. You have made her sad. Sad with your lies. You should not have lied to your friend. It is not as though you have so many friends left. Or any at all. Do you have any friends, Alice Kwagala? Why did you lie?

ALICE: Please go.

YUSEFU: But I have just arrived. (*Beat.*) Why did you lie to your friend?

ALICE: I did not kill him.

YUSEFU: Why do you lie now?

ALICE: I am not –

YUSEFU: Your lies have gotten you into trouble before and yet you continue to allow them to escape your lips. You lie so much that you make others lie as well. I lie to say that you are my niece and that I am your uncle and that I love you and this lie is like a poison in my mouth. But I will swallow this poison of a lie to find you. And I have. (*Beat.*) It was not difficult to find you. It was not easy; I am still an old man. No, not easy but not impossible. As you can see. There were so many places I had to look. Lists, organisations, support groups, centres. There is so much help for you killers.

ALICE: I did not kill him.

YUSEFU: Who is helping us? Eh? I have not held a gun. I have not hacked limbs off or beaten people to death – burned people to death. I have not burned down villages. Who helps us, those with clean hands? (*Beat.*) You have all of these wonderful books to hide behind. Books and lists and rehabilitation centres. They hide you, but only for a little while. (*Beat.*) Your mother thinks you are dead, the stupid woman. Or maybe she wishes that you were dead. Maybe that is how she sleeps at night, eh? But I knew that Alice Kwagala – I knew that you would be living.

ALICE: I did not...

YUSEFU: Your mother has so many beautiful grandchildren. Grandsons and granddaughters. Do you think that she would give me one of hers? It would only be fair. That is the least that you both owe me.

ALICE: Julius...

YUSEFU: I could pick out a boy. To replace my Julius. She has so many, she will not miss one. I will be kind to you and take one of the nephews that you have not met. One of the new ones; those that were born during the five years that you have been away. I will take one of those.

ALICE: Please do not hurt them.

YUSEFU: What do you care for your family? You lie and say that they are dead. Is it because you know that they will not have you back. They are afraid that you may slit their throats in the night just as you did to countless others. Other mothers, sisters, nieces.

ALICE: They know that I was a soldier.

YUSEFU: Do they know how many you killed? How much blood the ground has drank because of you?

ALICE is willing herself not to cry.

ALICE: It is not my fault that Julius was killed.

YUSEFU: He followed you everywhere in the village. You knew he would follow you into war.

ALICE: No. I begged them to let him go. I begged them to send Julius home.

YUSEFU: And yet it is he that is in the grave, not you. (*Beat.*) Did you bury him?

Silence.

So he does not even have a grave for his eight year-old body. Ach.

ALICE: There are many without graves.

YUSEFU: Julius will forever remain an eight year-old boy whereas today you are a seventeen year-old murderer. Some day, if you live these many years, you will be a seventy year-old murderer. While Julius will still be an eight year-old boy, a child. (*Pause.*) It was said that you had a child.

ALICE:

YUSEFU:

Beat.

Is it without a grave as well? Or perhaps it has a tiny one – shallow, that you had to dig with your hands. You would have had to have been quick. And quiet. Quick and quiet and without tears. A soldier does not have time to cry, does one?

Silence.

Yes, with your teenage hands. How old were you, fourteen? Fifteen? Did they bleed, your young hands, as you clawed at the earth?

Silence.

Did they?! I need to know that your hands are forever scarred. (*Beat.*) Please do not think that this makes everything even between us. No. While I am glad that you know the anguish of having your child die, you also had solace in burying that child.

RENA appears in the doorway, unnoticed by either of the two.

Did it die of hunger? Of thirst? Did it become ill with cholera? Or was it killed by a bullet meant for you? I must know. I know how the filth of your womb perished.

ALICE: It made me slow. (*Pause.*) If you want to be a living soldier, then you cannot be a slow one. I chose to fight because I saw things that the government was doing to our people. To my family and friends and I wanted to become a politician and to change things, but I was twelve. And no one listens to a child; not until that child has a gun in her hands. But no one listens to a dead child either. (*Beat.*) I had to survive.

YUSEFU:

ALICE: I had to. To survive. I have never had a boyfriend, but I have been a wife to so many. So many have been my husband. So many. (*Beat.*) I could not be slow. No.

Silence.

YUSEFU:

Beat. UNCLE YUSEFU laughs. ALICE realises that UNCLE YUSEFU did not know her secret.

ALICE:

YUSEFU: You love the taste of blood so much that you would kill your own child.

ALICE:

YUSEFU: Did you drown it? Smash its head with a rock? Smother it? What? Slit its throat? Any mother would die before letting her child lose its life. But you, Alice Kwagala. You are…

UNCLE YUSEFU notices RENA standing in the doorway. It is clear to him that she has heard everything. He smiles.

ALICE: Are we even now?

Beat.

YUSEFU: No. Not yet.

ALICE: No? What does that mean? (*Pause.*) What does it mean?!

ALICE notices RENA. She turns towards her friend. Silence.

YUSEFU: Now, now we are even. (*To RENA.*) Now you know the company that you keep.

In his smugness, UNCLE YUSEFU walks over to the books. Silence.

ALICE: Rena, I did not even give her a name. My mother has another granddaughter... She would not want to see me. Who would want –

RENA: 'My husband pours scorn
On Black People,'

ALICE: I am not –

RENA: 'He behaves like a hen
That eats its own eggs
A hen that should be imprisoned under a blanket.'

Beat. RENA continues.

'His eyes grow large
Deep black eyes'

RENA waits.

ALICE:

RENA: 'Ocol's eyes resemble those of the Nile Perch!
He becomes fierce'

ALICE takes up the poem, but in Acholi. They recite the poem together.

RENA / ALICE: 'Like a lioness with cubs,
 He begins to behave like a mad hyena.
 He says Black people are primitive
 And their ways are utterly harmful,
 Their dances mortal sins
 They are ignorant, poor and diseased!'

ALICE:

RENA:

Silence.

YUSEFU: What will my Julius know of schools? What will he know of books and pencils and playtime?

They both look at UNCLE YUSEFU.

What will he know of sitting beside his grandfather, reading poetry to his grandfather? What will he know of the magic of reciting wonderful, wonderful poetry?

As he talks, it is clear that UNCLE YUSEFU has been setting the books on fire.

(*To ALICE.*) There will be no more books for you to hide behind.

RENA: What are you doing?!

RENA grabs several of the burning books, trying to smother the flames.

YUSEFU: No more.

RENA: What are you doing?!

ALICE: Rena!

RENA can't keep up with UNCLE YUSEFU as he sets more books alight. ALICE goes to help her, but there are now too many books on fire and the fire is getting out of control. ALICE pulls at RENA, pulling her away from the books they are trying to save.

Rena!

SOL appears at the door. ALICE sees him.

ALICE: Help, Sol!

SOL: Rena!

SOL rushes into the school. He grabs hold of RENA, but she reaches out for ALICE.

RENA: Alice! Alice!

ALICE is trying to get UNCLE YUSEFU out, but he won't be pulled away from the burning books.

ALICE: Come! Please!

RENA: Alice!

SOL: Rena! Come on, Rena!

RENA struggles against SOL's pull, so SOL grabs holds of ALICE as well and finally pulls both RENA and ALICE out of the school.

SCENE 6

The charred remains of the schoolhouse.

SOL and OSCAR stand, looking at the devastation caused by the fire. SOL has burns, which are not severe, but have been bandaged. He looks at the remains of one of OSCAR's benches. SOL tries to pick it up, but it falls apart in his hands. Both men stare at the ashes of the bench. Beat. Then though he's obviously in pain, SOL continues to sort through the debris. OSCAR watches him.

RENA enters, carrying a rucksack. She too has burns that have been bandaged. OSCAR and SOL both see her, then look at each other. Beat. SOL goes back to work. OSCAR goes over to RENA.

OSCAR: You off?

RENA nods.

RENA: Blagged a ride to the airport.

OSCAR: Scared?

RENA: Shitless, actually.

OSCAR: Good. That means you at least care. (*Beat.*) They'll be glad to see you.

RENA: Maybe they won't.

OSCAR: No, maybe they won't.

RENA: Maybe I should stay, then.

OSCAR:

RENA:

Beat.

And here was me thinking I'd just be hanging out in the jungle.

OSCAR: I don't think I can do this anymore, Rena.

RENA: Oscar…

OSCAR: I don't think I can start over.

RENA sees that OSCAR is on the verge of tears.

The school –

RENA: Our school.

SOL, who was looking on, turns away.

It's better than a poke in the eye with a sharp stick.

OSCAR snorts. RENA looks around at the destroyed schoolhouse.

It shows we were here, Oscar. That we didn't do nothing.

Beat.

OSCAR: I'm too old for this shit.

RENA laughs. She looks at SOL, who is clearing away a desk.

He'll be okay.

SOL winces in pain. Both RENA and OSCAR rush over to him. SOL gestures for them to back away.

SOL: I've got it.

OSCAR stops in his attempt to assist SOL, but RENA takes hold of the other side of the desk.

I said I've got it.

OSCAR exits.

RENA: You should've stayed in hospital.

SOL shakes his head.

SOL: I'm fine.

RENA:

SOL:

RENA: Thanks for –

SOL: I've got things to get on with, Rena.

RENA: Thank you, Sol. Thank you.

Beat.

SOL: What makes you think Dad wants you back, anyway?

Beat.

RENA: He probably doesn't.

SOL scoffs.

But I have to prove to me that I can do this.

SOL: Prove what, that you're still Rena the misfit? Petty thief, racist, scrounger, ASBO menace – that's how they still see you, you know.

RENA: There's another Rena and Alice let me – (*Long pause.*) I don't have to let other people tell me who I am anymore. I need to figure out how I see myself

SOL shrugs.

You'd rather stand in front of bulldozers than stand your ground with Dad. You'd rather stay where a man burned to death than –

SOL: And do you know why?! 'Get proper job, Sol.' 'Don't tell people that, say something different.' 'We'll be dead and buried by the time you make a difference.' That shit makes me feel like my degree, my work, my – everything, my everything doesn't mean anything. I want to fly, Rena and you just want me to stay down. You think I'm owed to you; I belong to you. You don't let go. Don't let it rest. So down I stay. Blood does that. It drags you down. (*Beat.*) All these people in all these countries; them, I can let go of them. Because they don't ask me to give up on my dreams.

RENA:

SOL:

RENA:

SOL: I'm needed here, Rena. I'm needed here.

Beat. As RENA turns to go, ALICE arrives. She too has a few bandaged burns.

RENA: Alice?

ALICE: You are going home today, yes?

ALICE looks at SOL and smiles. RENA turns to her brother. SOL looks away and goes back to clearing things away.

RENA: Thank you, Sol.

SOL continues to work. RENA and ALICE exit, but SOL doesn't realise this. He holds up a book that's damaged, but still intact.

SOL: Rena? Can you tell Mum that I –

SOL turns to find that he is alone. He flicks through the book then carefully puts it out of the way.

End.

By the same author

Compact Failure
9781840025187

WWW.OBERONBOOKS.COM